OVERCOMING

WOMEN'S STORIES OF RESILIENCE, FAITH AND SELF-DISCOVERY IN A PANDEMIC

OLUWAKEMI AKAGWU, ADEMILOLA BILEWOMO

Dedication

To our mothers who taught us to overcome.

Table of Content

THE BOOK IN YOUR HANDS

Oluwakemi Akagwu

I wake up most days around 5 a.m. As my mind embraces consciousness, I often have a flood of ideas. They are usually thoughts on how to solve a nagging problem, or audacious ideas about some project. Usually, I grab the thoughts giving solutions to my challenges, then pause to think about the feasibility of implementing some of the other ideas.

One morning in May 2020, I woke up and began my usual sequence of filtering through my ideas. In the previous two months, Nigeria had been on lockdown to curb the spread of COVID-19. It was a time of gloom and uncertainty. It had become my family's routine to watch the news for daily updates on the number of new COVID-19 cases and deaths. The outlook of that day in May was not any different. We were all going to sit at home and tune in to the news for updates on the pandemic. As I sorted through my early morning ideas, one of them filtered its way to the top.

Why don't I write a collection of stories focused on

It was not the first time I had thought about writing a book. Reading is my favourite pastime, and I remember my childhood attempts at writing a book or two. However, with the busyness of adulthood, this aspiration had taken backstage. The temptation came to discard this idea, but I decided to have none of it. To ensure I didn't talk myself out of embarking on this journey, I quickly sent a WhatsApp message to a friend to seek her collaboration. Her positive response came back some hours later, and so began the journey of making the book you have in your hands.

We quickly got to work and set up a plan to get published within six months. We both had a bit of time on our hands: we were both in the middle of career changes and so were not working full-time jobs at the time. The lockdown had brought many other facets of life to a standstill. We reckoned that everyone was at home and would quickly respond to our request for stories. We drafted a list of names and sent emails asking for stories. We also set up a website and waited expectantly for the stories to flood in. To our surprise and disappointment, we got just a trickle. Only two people responded to our request. This was despite the expression of interest we had received from many of the women we contacted.

We realised that we needed to change tactics if we were going to get the stories we wanted. We decided to run with the idea of co-developing the stories with women who had indicated an interest in being part of the project. So, we scheduled video calls to interview contributors living around the world. We followed up the calls by long hours transcribing and developing these interviews into stories. We also had follow-up dialogues to ensure that the stories truly captured their experiences and the messages they wanted to pass across.

The months went by, the lockdown ended, and life continued amidst the pandemic. We both got new career opportunities and started working full-time. We struggled with childcare, online schooling, work deadlines, maintaining our physical and emotional health while living through the pandemic. The temptation to quit writing came several times. There were weeks when we did not get any writing done. We found that this struggle was reflective of the stories shared with us by many of our contributors. We remained determined that this would not be an unfinished project.

We got contributions from women across the globe and in different phases of life. From a little girl starting a business to women embracing loneliness or struggling to balance the demands of work and childcare, here are stories of women's lives interrupted by the COVID-19 pandemic. As we listened to the interviews and read the stories, we were inspired by the resilience displayed by each woman in overcoming the challenges and uncertainty of the pandemic. We settled on writing stories with a positive tone in celebration of the ability of women to rise above life's challenges.

In writing these stories, we do not belittle the pain and loss our contributors and other women have suffered because of the pandemic. Rather, we are turning the lens on opportunities to ride above uncertainty, pain, and loss. We hope reading this book brings a message of hope to someone: that though life is messy, and there are inevitable changes in plans and timelines, they can still overcome. We hope these stories will inspire you to keep moving and holding on to hope.

About Oluwakemi

Oluwakemi is a medical doctor whose practice is focused on public health. She loves using her skills to help communities access and utilise life-saving health services. She loves listening to music, reading good books, and taking in nature's beauty while on walks or visiting new places. She lives in Abuja, Nigeria with her amazing husband, Cyril, and two children.

ON THE FRONTLINE

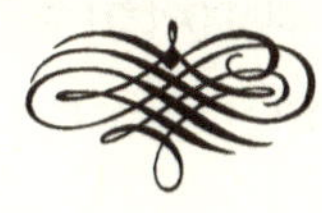

Joanna Gbotoe

Leaving my comfort zone

My name is Joanna; I was born and brought up in Liberia.

I spent a large part of my childhood with an American missionary couple. My values of selfless service, hard work, and determination were born out of their discipline and training. The American couple inspired me to become a nurse and serve humanity through my career. Following my passion and saving lives require overcoming the instinct to throw in the towel. I must keep showing up for the patients who count on me.

In 2018, after working for over 18 years as a nurse in Liberia, I began considering getting some international experience. During this time, I came across a job advertisement for a position with the UN Clinic in Goma, in the Democratic Republic of Congo (DRC). A quick review of the requirements alerted me that the role would mean stretching out of my comfort zone. I would have to travel to another country, learn the common language, and assimilate the culture. The DRC is a Francophone country and had been at war for many years. It was also a country struggling with Ebola. But the particulars of the DRC were not far from that of my home country, Liberia. I had worked as a nurse and survived through 14 years of Liberia's civil war and the anguish of the 2014 Ebola epidemic, which claimed thousands of lives in Liberia and Sierra Leone.

I decided that going to the DRC was an opportunity worth taking. So I applied, interviewed for the position, and landed the job. One of the things that struck me when I arrived in the DRC was the beautiful geography of Goma. The beauty, however, was not without its beast. My office is situated on the banks of Kivu Lake, which has an active volcano to its north.

Despite similarities between the DRC and Liberia regarding war and epidemics, I quickly realised that our cultures were different. So, I sought to understand the people's way of life; I enrolled in French classes to bridge the language barrier. Work at the clinic in Goma was routine. Daily activities revolved around providing primary outpatient care for staff, guiding newcomers to update immunization status, and supporting newcomers to adjust to life and healthcare in the country. Emergency cases were referred to the UN Level three facility. At the close of work, I would return to my apartment and spend the rest of the hours resting, watching TV, and catching up with my family in Liberia and the US.

The DRC faced its largest outbreak of Ebola between 2018 and 2020. It started in the North Kivu Province and spread to Ituri and South Kivu. By March 2020, there had been over 2,000 deaths, but the number of new cases had reduced significantly; there were hopes that the outbreak would soon end.

Against the backdrop of the battle with Ebola, I watched as the news headlines began to carry stories of a new virus that had originated in China and was spreading rapidly around the world. In early March, the DRC recorded its index case of COVID-19. It was a man who had recently returned to Kinshasa from France. One COVID-19 case multiplied to five patients and one death within a short time. The DRC was the first country in the region to report a case of COVID-19. Other countries in the area responded swiftly by closing their land borders with us. By April 2020, there was a complete lockdown, allowing for no movements in or out of the DRC. Cases rapidly climbed from less than a hundred in March to over

2,000 in April.

I had planned a vacation in Liberia in March 2020, but I had to cancel. Staff who were out of the country could not return because of the border closures. With the gravity of the situation settling in, plans were set in motion for those who could work remotely. However, being an essential worker, I had to report physically at the clinic. Infection control measures were put in place at the clinic and daily broadcasts were made to advise all staff; people with COVID-like symptoms were asked to stay home and call in for help. With COVID-19 cases popping up and rapidly spreading across more regions than had been affected by Ebola, panic spread. In time, we saw staff members come down with COVID-19 and become critically ill, needing oxygen. We moved them to referral centres.

Many health workers like me also contracted COVID-19. As close associates developed symptoms, we became short-staffed. This put more pressure on the work roster and on the physical and mental wellbeing of available staff. The combination of loneliness, uncertainty, and the emotional turmoil of seeing critically ill COVID-19 patients started taking a toll on me. Every time I had to see or transfer a suspected COVID-19 case, I would fear that I would be next.

Eventually, I went into self-isolation because a colleague I closely worked with contracted the disease. Thus began my panic attacks and a blood pressure that ran high.

I realized I had to fight to make it through and not give in. I remembered my family back home in Liberia – my mother, who was not feeling too well, and other family members who depended on me for help. I encouraged myself and told myself I could go through the storm. I also drew strength from my experiences as a nurse during the Liberian Civil War. I had worked with the International Red Cross in an emergency unit. I had attended to thousands of wounded soldiers and civilians, putting their needs above my physical and emotional needs at the time. I reckoned if I could get through that, I could survive COVID-19 as well. Mustering my inner strength and will, I pushed back and overcame anxiety and despair. I also got help with medications to bring my blood pressure under control.

Through this crisis, I have been reminded that my attitude and response to life situations and people go a long way in determining if life is good and happy. This is especially true when life throws you events that you have no control over, such as having to live through a civil war or pandemic.

About Joanna

Joanna is a registered nurse with a public health background. She is currently working as a United Nations Medical Volunteer in the DRC.

She is married and a mother of two boys. Her hobbies are cooking, antiquing, travelling and making people laugh.

A PANDEMIC
TURNED PERSONAL

Ify E.

An unfolding pandemic

There are years and life events that redefine who we are - when our foundation is tested, and we leave such seasons a different person. The year 2020 was one of those seasons for me. I remember crafting my dreams and aspirations for the year 2020 in December 2019. I was excited, as I anticipated what the new year would bring. Never did I, in my wildest dreams, anticipate the way the year eventually unfolded. As 2020 began, the news of a new virus discovered in China called COVID-19 started making waves around the globe. As a journalist, I attended a workshop and briefing session organized by the World Health Organisation (WHO) to raise awareness about the novel virus. I remember sitting unperturbed through the sessions and thinking the virus would never get to Nigeria.

Following the workshop, I published an article on COVID-19, and I continued to watch as the pandemic ravaged other parts of the world. I followed the story as the number of cases increased worldwide. I watched stupefied as other African countries recorded their cases, and then the unimaginable happened - Nigeria had her first case! I remember hearing the breaking news of COVID-19 in Nigeria but still believing that somehow, all of this was far off.

Diagnosed with COVID-19

One of the reasons I felt untouchable by COVID-19 was that I wasn't working a regular 9-5 job. As a freelance journalist, I only went out for a few hours every day to cover events or host a radio program and then write my reports at home. Hence, I reasoned I was not likely to come in contact with the virus. I never thought that the pandemic would personally touch me, but it did. Indeed, everyone in my nuclear family had a brush with the virus.

I recall vividly, like yesterday, the journey to being diagnosed. I was hosting a radio program when I started having bouts of cough while on air, so I had to go off air for a bit. After the show, I spoke to a doctor friend who was involved in the COVID-19 response. She advised me to get tested and quickly had a response team sent to my house to collect my sample. The day my sample was taken, the personnel came decked in protective gear with an ambulance and blaring sirens.

After the sample collection began a period of suspense. After four days, I could not bear the suspense any longer, so I made contact. I remember getting the shock of my life as I was informed that I had tested positive for COVID-19. I waited so long for my results because my sample had been collected by the FCT response team, but since my residential address was in another state, my result had been sent to that state's team for further action.

The next few hours after I received my test result passed in a blur. I am not sure I slept the night I got the result, but I made it to the next day and awaited the team to take me to the isolation centre. The team arrived in an ambulance with sirens blaring and much hullabaloo. They explained that samples would have to be taken from every member of my household because they had been in close contact with me and maybe infected too. As I entered the ambulance, a strong sense of fear enveloped me and I panicked. I looked across the ambulance and met the eyes of my travel companion. He was an eight-year-old boy who was also being taken to the isolation centre. For the brief moment our eyes met, I saw the fear in his eyes. He quickly looked away and remained sullen throughout our journey. As the ambulance moved out of my driveway and wound its way down the streets, a million thoughts came crashing through my mind like the waves of a storm-tossed sea. My thoughts flashed back to the sight of my three-year-old daughter crying as she was dragged out of my reach as I was led to the waiting ambulance. I battled with the fear of other members of my household being diagnosed with COVID-19. I was also worried about how my three-year-old daughter would cope without me.

Life in an isolation centre

At the isolation centre, I was led to the room which would be my home for the next couple of weeks. I was soon joined by my husband, my two children, and two relatives who lived with us because they all tested positive. To the credit of the health workers in the isolation centre, everyone was kind and supportive. The nurses came around to check us regularly; they always had encouraging words. I drew strength from their care and friends who formed my support system as we faced the challenging weeks ahead.

Not long after, my symptoms started worsening. The cough bouts became more frequent, longer and left me breathless. I was also reacting to some of the drugs I was receiving, so I vomited several times a day. One night, I threw up so many times that I became very weak and dehydrated. The health workers quickly gave me intravenous fluids, but I had to be pricked up to fifteen times before they could find the right vein. At that point, I thought that I would not live, but I survived.

Another challenge that I faced was caring for the children, especially my three-year-old. Being young and energetic, the children felt trapped and restless in the confinement of our isolation room. Getting the children to take their drugs was also another matter altogether. My husband and I had to exercise our creativity and imagination to keep them occupied and distracted every day.

As the days rolled into weeks, our tests were repeated. We were shocked when the results were returned, and my three-year-old was negative while the rest of us were still positive. She was immediately discharged from the isolation centre, and we sent her to stay with a family friend. For the second time in a few weeks, I had to watch my daughter cry as she was whisked away from me while I watched helplessly. The separation was not easy for anyone, and I remember how we all cried together that last night she spent with us at the isolation centre. When my daughter was discharged, I found myself spiralling down into depression. I had been tested twice since my admission, and both results returned positive. It did not help that around me were other patients in the same state. I remember a lady in the room next to ours who we could always hear crying as each test she had was returned positive. At this time, the guidelines had not been updated to discharge patients after two weeks in isolation, so everyone was sentenced to stay in the isolation centre until they had a negative result.

The day finally came when all of us tested negative and were discharged! It felt surreal that the ordeal had ended, and we could all go back home to continue life again as a family.

A life of gratitude

I now look at my life with a great sense of gratitude. I have diabetes which is considered a risk factor for severe disease. Diabetes raises the risk of dying from COVID significantly, but I survived. However, not everyone was so lucky. Indeed, I lost a friend and mentor to COVID-19.

I am immensely thankful for my faith in God which was instilled in me as a pastor's child, and the numerous people who stood by me, helping me through the trying moments.

This experience has further bolstered my belief that life is about people. From friends who always had an encouraging word, to the friends who my daughter stayed with while we were still in isolation– the relationships we built over the years played a great role in getting us through the ordeal. The year threw me a curveball, but I can say I have emerged a stronger and more grateful person.

About Ify

Ify is a development communications expert who is building a career in the development sector with a strong passion for health communication. She is presently studying for her doctoral degree in Development Communication. She is happily married and blessed with two lovely children. She loves spending quality time with her family, listening to music, and doing what makes her happy.

JOURNEY TO MOTHERHOOD

Raquel Chun

I was raised in a village called Roaring Creek in the Cayo District of Belize, northwest of Belmopan City, the capital city of Belize. The village derives its name from the small creek that borders the village which joins one of the largest rivers in my country- the Belize River. Growing up, my mother was my greatest inspiration. She had eight of us (two of us died when they were toddlers), and she poured her love and energy into raising us all. She worked very hard and pushed us – especially her girls - to aspire to become the best we could be. I remain inspired by how much she overcame in life. She had humble beginnings, did not have the opportunity to have an education, and left her home while she was very young to start building a life of her own. Despite this, she pulled through the various difficulties and made something great of her life. Her passing in 2018 remains the lowest moment of my life.

I saw my mother's hard work and sacrifices for her

children, which I also aspire to do. I always knew becoming a mother would be a great source of pride for me, as I would be responsible for inspiring a little human - just as my mother inspired me. My idea was to ensure I was fully prepared to embark on the journey of motherhood before starting a family. Whenever we discussed having children, I always told my partner we needed to make sure that we knew what we would be taking on, because having a child is a lot of responsibility.

When I did eventually get pregnant, it was an unplanned and unexpected event. I had received a studentship for a PhD in the United Kingdom (UK) and was shuttling between the UK and Belize at the time. My thoughts had been to hold off having a baby until towards the end of my program. To my surprise, in September 2019, I found out I was pregnant. In the weeks preceding my discovery, I noticed that I was always hungry, even at very odd times. Initially, I attributed my increased appetite to stress, but I soon realized I had not seen my period in two months. I finally took a pregnancy test that turned out positive and visited my doctor. She confirmed that I was about six weeks gone. I was in Belize at the time, but I had to return to the UK three months later to continue working on my PhD. I was fortunate not to have any nausea and vomiting associated with early pregnancy. Through my time in the UK, I accessed antenatal care facilities through the NHS.

As 2020 began, I started hearing stories of a disease ravaging Asia. Next, I began seeing signs at the hospital when I went for antenatal care: posters everywhere urging people to clean their hands and maintain good health in the face of the epidemic that could come to Europe. As things continued to progress, unnecessary visits to the hospitals were discouraged. The UK announced its possible lockdown in early March 2020 – the virus had entered the UK from Italy and was spreading. I was due to have my baby in April and had planned to travel back to Belize to have him there. With the impending lockdown in the UK, I had to quickly change my travel plans and return to Belize in mid-March. My brother, who worked in the Ministry of Health in Belize, was very concerned about me traveling: but I desperately needed to get back home. When I got to Belize, I had to be in quarantine as a precaution because we did not understand this new virus. So, for three weeks after my return, I was locked up, on my own, in my house. It was emotionally draining and mentally demanding, but I was just happy to be home and close to family.

I was due to have my baby in April; Belize had gone into lockdown in late March and extended into April and beyond. Life was suddenly not normal anymore. I still went for my antenatal visits, but I had to be very careful. My initial plan had been to give birth at a public hospital because of the lower costs and experienced staff. However, with COVID-19 and a lockdown in effect, I decided to opt for birth at a private hospital instead - especially because I expected to have a vaginal birth. I had become afraid of going to the public hospital because they had managed some COVID-19 patients, and numbers were increasing slowly. I feared for my newborn.

During one of my routine antenatal checks at the tail end of my pregnancy, the doctor discovered that my baby's heartbeat was slower than it should be. They advised an emergency caesarean section to save my baby's life. I found myself making quick decisions, unprepared for such an event. In less than thirty minutes, I had to decide if I wanted them to cut me. I had to sign waivers that I barely understood because I did not fully understand what was happening. My doctor said they needed to take the child out because he might not survive another hour or normal delivery. I would find out later that his umbilical cord had developed too short, and as he was descending in preparation for birth, the placenta was being ripped off the uterus, limiting the amount of oxygen that he was getting. My partner worked in another town and had just travelled back the day before, so I had to place a call across to let him know what was happening while I was prepped for surgery.

It is crazy how quickly things can turn around. My sister accompanied me to the hospital that day, and we had planned to order takeout at a restaurant on our way home. But instead of getting takeout, I was given an epidural and cut to deliver my baby boy. My sister was the first family member to hold him. When I was still lying on the operating table, she put him near my face so that I could see him, and I remember exclaiming, "Oh, he is here!"

After the surgery, I could barely move because every move was painful. At some point, they put my baby close to me so that he could smell me and get used to my body heat. They tried to make him start feeding, but I could not do that because I could not move my hands, so they held him in place as he searched for his food. It was a very sudden introduction to motherhood. My partner made it to the hospital about three hours after the baby's birth to meet his son and me.

We returned home a day later, and I settled into the life of a mother. My sister, cousin, and mother-in-law were very helpful, sleeping in some nights. Getting this help was not without some risks. During one of her trips, my cousin went to an offshore island for a brief visit. While she was there, several COVID-19 cases were reported. So, as a precaution, we decided for her not to come to our house for three weeks in case of any risk of exposure. There were fears that she could be infected, that other family members and I could be at risk.

As my son grew, I adjusted to raising an infant during a pandemic. There were many experiences I wished for but could not have. I come from a close-knit family, and we weren't able to have them gather to meet him or visit us occasionally. I did not get to have a baptism party for my son at three or six months or a family gathering to mark it. I had to limit the time I spent outdoors with him. We also had to cope with the dynamics of the family living apart. My partner was an essential health worker, and the clinic where he worked was in the south of Belize, where internet connectivity is poor. With my PhD work ongoing, I had to stay with my sister in my home village to access the internet readily. We limited travel between our locations to reduce our son's exposure to COVID-19.

As my son turned one in April 2021, COVID-19 restrictions were still in effect, but with more allowance. We took the opportunity of his christening to honour my mother's love for her faith and do a small celebration with close family. Belize enjoyed a long period with low numbers of cases in the early to the middle part of 2021, so we were able to take him out more often, but nowhere far and not for too long. We went on quick trips to the grocery store, to the open outside markets, and occasionally, to a restaurant. There were no trips to other countries yet and no national celebrations to look forward to. Before COVID-19, my family would sometimes take overnight trips to border towns in Mexico and Guatemala and even the cayes on the coast of Belize. With the pandemic, these were luxuries that were no longer possible to enjoy.

My son and I moved to southern Belize at the end of June 2021 so that I could undertake a second year of fieldwork. It was a big decision, but Belize had kept the number of COVID-19 cases very low, and we hoped this would continue.

In August 2021, the third wave of COVID-19 began in Belize, with numbers increasing daily. Vaccines were available, but the vaccination campaign contended with the rise of anti-vaxxers and conspiracy theorists. The rapidly changing medical advice on the COVID vaccines did not help the matter. I had tried to get vaccinated in June but had been informed that they were not administering the vaccine to breastfeeding mothers. I checked again in July 2021 when I got to southern Belize and was informed that studies had not shown that the vaccines had any adverse effects on breastfeeding mothers or their babies. So, I got my first shot. I had close calls where I encountered people who were exposed to the virus. We had an especially close call via my babysitter when her mother and sister tested positive for the virus. Consequently, she stayed away for two weeks, but the time had to be extended to a month when additional cases cropped up in her family. While she was away, I saw how close my baby and me had come to contracting this deadly virus that no one really knew about.

It always hits me how different the world was at the beginning of my pregnancy and how everything has changed in my son's first year of life. I have come to appreciate the little things one takes for granted, like gathering with family or travelling freely. We live our lives and expect things always to remain the same.

Now, COVID-19 has shown the world how rapidly things can change.

About Raquel

Raquel Chun is an ardent lover of nature, fueled by the beauty of the environment she grew up in. She is from a large and loving family with many amazing nieces and nephews. Raquel is also a great believer in education and hopes to contribute to the positive development of Belize in her chosen field.

THE BALANCING ACT

Oluwaseyi Adegbulugbe

"Mummy, I'm bored!"

I turned from my laptop to meet my daughter's earnest gaze.

"Mummy, I'm bored," she whined again, probably for the hundredth time that day. "Sweetie, why don't you try and create activities for yourself?" I asked and received a vehement "No!" in response. I sighed in exasperation and tried to calm myself while wondering what to do with my six-year-old daughter. This same conversation, in various forms, had repeated itself almost every day since we found ourselves stuck at home because of the COVID-19 pandemic.

As a busy career woman working for a Non-Governmental Organization, I had been able to bring some sanity into the art of juggling expectations at home and work by leveraging the support systems I had built. I am the mum who uses the school bus to transport my two children to and from school and puts them in extracurricular activities to engage them. Fortunately, my mother lives in the same city as me and is always willing to care for my children when I am not around.

Life was busy, but I was succeeding in the balancing act. But nobody warned me that a balancing act is like a row of dominoes or a stack of cards; it only takes one element to tip over, and everything can go wildly out of sync.

At first, when talk of COVID-19 started making rounds, I bought into the myth that Nigeria would be spared. I reasoned this was not the first flu of epidemic proportions in recent years. After all, Nigeria had not been significantly affected by all the past pandemics. This, too, would pass, like all others before it. However, as things evolved over the weeks, I realized that this situation would be different.

In the first quarter of 2020, the index COVID case in Nigeria was identified in Lagos. As though they were waiting for who to go first, cases popped up in Abuja, and lockdowns were instituted. So, the cascade of unfolding events disrupted my support system. Schools were shut, and my children were stuck at home. We stopped going to my mother's house to minimise her exposure to the virus.

Alongside the increasing burden of childcare, I found myself having to work from home. Though our physical offices had been shut, we still had to deliver on assigned tasks. So, I found myself in a flurry of activities; rushing from one zoom meeting to the next, responding to work-related emails, typing furiously on my laptop to meet a deadline while sometimes attending to a crying child, preparing another snack, and rocking a child who had decided no one else would carry him but me. I found myself getting physically and emotionally exhausted as I was literally being dragged in a hundred different directions at once.

During the early chaotic weeks of my new normal, I learnt the value of emotional support. Emotional support, put simply, is having someone to talk to, who understands and allows us to let out steam. There was a Saturday I felt that I had reached my tipping point. Under pressure and stress, I had taken some actions that I was not proud of and was on a guilt trip. The lockdown was easing at this point, and I had bundled my kids over to my mother's place. However, I was still faced with a load of housework, and my blinking laptop light was a constant reminder of work that I needed to attend to. As I tried to juggle my guilt, housework, and career that Saturday, my cousin called in on the phone. As we got talking, I found myself in tears as I narrated my ordeal to her. She listened to my ranting and encouraged me to offload. When we finished talking, nothing about my situation had changed, but I felt much better. I left that call feeling much lighter and better able to face my day. I realized that providing a listening, non-judgmental ear is one way to help one another surmount our challenges.

Most of us try to be superwomen every day. We wake up each morning, and our minds automatically roll to all the tasks we must carry out, usually for everyone but ourselves. Then we find ourselves on guilt trips when everything doesn't work as we hoped. We need a safe space to listen to each other and tell ourselves the truth: balancing the various dimensions of life is not easy. I have realised that it's ok not to be perfect; sometimes, it's ok to feel overwhelmed and drop the ball. What is more important is that we don't get stuck there but continue moving forward.

Moving forward may mean paying more attention to your emotional and physical health, re-evaluating priorities, or even taking the bold step of a career or job change. For me, moving forward has been rediscovering who I am, learning to take each day as it comes, building my trust in God, and intentionally taking time to bond with my family. So, despite all the challenges, I am glad I got the time for introspection and to understand myself better.

About Oluseyi

Oluseyi Adegbulugbe is a public health practitioner experienced in health preventive and promotive programs with a focus on gender and adolescent girls/young women. She is passionate about reducing inequities that limit women and girls from harnessing their full potential.

Her fun side includes singing in a classical choir and all forms of shopping. She is blessed with two awesome children, whom she absolutely adores.

MIEBI'S QUEST

Miebi Feboke

✳

narrated by Ademilola Bilewomo

As the first wave of the COVID-19 pandemic hit Nigeria, the government's initial response was to close primary and secondary schools early. Though many Nigerians welcomed the development, it was particularly challenging for parents, especially mothers. I remember having several conversations with my friends on how challenging it was for the children to transition into virtual learning, or how tough it seemed to earn a living while teaching and caring for the children. It was during one of these conversations with a friend that I learnt about Miebi, her daughter.

Like many children her age, Miebi was home and bored with virtual schooling. Between attending school online and coping with boredom, she requested an Android tablet from her parents. Her parents had responded that she had to come up with the money to get the tablet. Thus began Miebi's quest for a novel idea to make money.

Hardly anyone would have thought that a five-year-old would have considered earning money an important challenge. While I focused on the challenges of doing business during a pandemic, Miebi focused on the goal. Perhaps, in her five-year-old mind, she asked herself what she could do to make the money for her tablet.

Miebi was not the only one faced with the challenge of earning enough money to buy a tablet. Her two elder brothers had also decided that they too wanted Android tablets, and their parents had set them on the same challenge. The boys came up with quick-fix solutions that could fetch them money. One of Miebi's brothers, for instance, decided that he would do home chores over a period to earn the money he needed. Their mum laughed it off and explained that house chores were required of them as members of the family; they would have to do something else to make the money. Miebi, however, was resolute in her quest. After careful thought, she came up with an idea.

"I want to make and sell beaded jewellery," Miebi said to her mother. Caught unawares, Miebi's mother prodded further to see if indeed her daughter was certain about her mission. It was little wonder that the five-year-old had caught her mum off-guard. Miebi had not made jewellery before, and she had not had prior discussions with an adult on such ventures. Therefore, it was a big surprise for her mother to see that Miebi had thought about her idea thoroughly.

Perhaps, it was her innocence or lack of life experience, but Miebi was unperturbed by her lack of skills for bead making. She decided she could learn the skill. With her parent's assistance, Miebi watched YouTube videos to learn the craft. Her parents were surprised at their daughter's maturity and wisdom at such a young age. More so, Miebi had already figured out that she needed to have customers buy her beads; indeed, she had even worked out a plan for sales. With her father's help, Miebi marketed her bead jewellery on Facebook, Instagram, and to family members and friends. Miebi's craft won the hearts of several people, and within a week, she had raised enough money to buy her tablet.

It was not just Miebi's ability to come up with her own business that warmed my heart; her dedication to achieving her goals is a lesson worth learning. Still having a diligent attitude and dedication to her craft, Miebi sought out new designs by asking her parents to help her search for more designs.

Surprisingly, when Miebi reached her goal, she did not

close her business. Instead, she aimed for another goal. This time, she wanted to raise enough funds to help children in need. However, as time passed and physical school resumed, Miebi redirected her energies and time to her studies. Nonetheless, she has chosen to continue focusing on her bead-making enterprise during school holidays.

Despite the gloom that came with COVID-19, Miebi taught me that even in the most challenging circumstances, we could decide how to respond to what life doles us. Rather than give up or choose defeat, I can focus on the goal and seek ways to reach it – even if it means learning a new skill.

About Miebi

Miebi is fun-loving and energetic. When she is not engrossed in schoolwork or making beads, she loves to role play as a salon/spa owner and hairdresser or learn to sew (she has completed her first class at sewing school). She recently got a yellow belt in Taekwondo and is trying her hand out at gymnastics. She is also learning to play the recorder and piano.

She lives in Abuja, Nigeria, with her parents, three brothers, and a pet dog.

LEADING THROUGH THE STORM

Jamila Faniyi

I discovered my love for construction and building during my teenage years. Technical drawing was one of my best subjects in secondary school. I was not just good at it; I enjoyed it immensely.

With this background, I naturally opted to study architecture at university. I wrote the required exams and sought placement at the Ahmadu Bello University, Zaria. When the university released its admission lists, I was admitted into Building instead of Architecture. Though Building had not been my first choice, I proceeded to study the course since it was closely related to architecture. So began my journey of working in the building and construction industry.

As a woman, climbing the professional ladder in a male-dominated profession hasn't been easy. Battles are fought on all levels: from gaining enough respect to being taken seriously in meetings to dealing with the workers on the field who believe a woman belongs in the kitchen and has no right to supervise their work. I joined my organization immediately after I finished my National Youth Service. I joined as entry-level staff but rose within five years to head my first department and, over time, assumed other leadership roles. When the business started a new subsidiary organization, I was moved to work there as the pioneer employee. A few months later, a leadership crisis arose within the new organization, and I was called upon to fill the gap. Since then, I have risen to become Chief Operations Officer (COO) and a member of the main organization management team.

Though the journey has had its ups and downs, I am grateful for the support I received from the organisation's leadership, which enabled me to grow and have some flexibility to attend to family needs.

My leadership journey started in my twenties. In my early years in leadership, many contractors did not take me seriously. They often attempted to sideline me in decision-making. Letters that should have been addressed to me would be addressed to the Chief Executive Officer (CEO), a man, instead of me. There were also subtle attempts to undermine my authority, as they constantly took to cross-check my decisions with the organisation's CEO before acting on them. It also didn't help that I was often the only female voice in the boardroom. Thankfully, my CEO strongly supported me. He never overruled my decisions. Instead, he would revert to me and stand by whatever decisions we made. With time, contractors and business partners learnt to accept that they had to deal with me if anything would get done. I have also seen the boardroom transform over time to have many more women in leadership roles.

The year 2020 was supposed to be my year of "freedom". I had been working hard building both my career and my family and had reached a point where I believed I could take a vacation and do things for myself without the kids or work barging in. I was looking forward to a time when I could just be myself and do some silly and crazy stuff with friends. 2020 was the year I and some of my friends would turn forty. So, we were all looking forward to starting our new decade with a vacation. Unfortunately, COVID-19 happened. Not only did my vacation not happen, but I now had to chart a leadership course in waters I had not navigated before.

I felt the effect of COVID-19 on many fronts. It hit close when I lost a cousin residing in the United States. It seemed like a bad dream when we received the news of her death. She had been young, vibrant, and full of life. She was neither elderly nor had any health issues; this made her death more difficult to come to terms with.

I had health issues. I had just been diagnosed with hypothyroidism and found out I was pregnant. With the lockdown, restriction of movement and fear of the unknown, many hospitals offered only skeletal services. Hence, getting consultation and treatment with a specialist became a challenge. The combination of hypothyroidism and early pregnancy left me feeling tired and drained a lot of the time.

I also had to adjust to the new normal of working from home and not stepping out of the house for days. I had always been on the move, from dashing out early in the morning to beat Lagos traffic, to catching up with one meeting or the other on my schedule. My days were usually a flurry of movement and activities. Now I had to adjust to doing everything while sitting down and staring at my laptop for hours. From dealing with my kids bumping into virtual meetings to the cackles of my geese or barks of my dogs in the background when I was on work calls, I gradually honed the art of working virtually.

As a leader, I had to look beyond my pain and discomfort

to watch for the welfare of my organization and staff. There were tough decisions to be made and staff morale to maintain if the organization would remain strong. During the arduous journey of leading an organization navigating the uncertainty of the future, three things were key for me: communication, quick adaptability, and resilience. During the tough times of the lockdown in Nigeria, I prioritized open lines of conversation with all staff. We had a reach-out program during which the human resource team called every staff member to find out how they were doing. We also assured them that we were doing everything to ensure the business remained on its feet and jobs were not lost. In addition, we asked unit managers to reach out to members of their teams. We maintained our regular meetings, which meant everyone had to embrace technology to participate in virtual discussions.

While moving from physical to virtual meetings came easily, some other organizational processes required more adaptation, patience and effort. For instance, we found our procurement process taking longer than usual because staff had to get around receiving necessary approvals via multiple emails instead of moving files physically as done previously. Virtual meetings also had to replace physical site visits, and it took some time to master how this could be done effectively.

A big issue that we had to deal with at the management level was declining revenue. During the lockdowns, construction projects were largely suspended, which translated to a loss of income. April and May 2020 were our most challenging months, and everyone had to have their salaries cut. By the third quarter of 2020, business began to pick up as the lockdowns and movement restrictions were lifted.

As I navigated what leadership looks like in a pandemic, a lot of learning and unlearning went on simultaneously on the home front. Like many career women in Nigeria, I had hired a domestic staff to help with household chores. This had worked fine over the years. However, she had resigned, and we were in the process of hiring someone else when the lockdown started. I was suddenly faced with having to take up more house chores while figuring out how to lead and work from home effectively. Initially, it was tricky getting the house organized without the support I had before. But everyone (from my husband to my three older children) pitched in, making it easier. We knew that all tasks were important, but urgent tasks had to be done first while the others were done later. Through this, I saw my children become more responsible, as everyone could see how doing or not doing assigned chores affected the household as a unit. With everyone stuck at home, each family member gained deeper insight into the habits and personalities of other family members. I laugh as I write this, but you think you know someone until you are locked down with them. I got to know things about my children and my husband for the first time. Conflicts arose, but we were forced to face them, talk about them and resolve them, since we had nowhere to go. In all, it was a period of growth and bonding for us all. My husband was particularly super during this time – patient and understanding.

I have come to realize that life will always have challenges that we need to solve, learn from and grow to do better. Each season of life comes with its unique challenges, which we must conquer. Situations will rarely present perfectly, but the onus is on us to navigate them and make things work. Seeing things this way has helped me through this pandemic.

About Jamila

Jamila is an Executive Director in Construction Kaiser, an indigenous construction company in Nigeria. She is the Managing Director of M&E Kaiser Limited, which specialises in mechanical and electrical installations.

She began her career in construction as a planning engineer in Construction Kaiser Limited and now has over sixteen years of unique experience in civil and MEPF construction planning, procurement, logistics and general project management. She has worked in both operations and management levels.

She holds a bachelor's degree in building from Ahmadu Bello University, Zaria, a master's degree in Construction Management from the University of Lagos, is certified in Advanced Management by the Lagos Business School with lots of training both locally and internationally including Harvard Business School, Boston. She has spearheaded several projects of clients from fruition to completion and consistently seeks to demonstrate excellence in leadership.

EMBRACING MY MUSIC

Kasandra Vegas

My musical roots

Music has always been a part of my life. As a child in Samoa, some of my favourite times in school were when we would assemble in the auditorium and sing songs of our history. Music is such a big part of Samoan culture, and it is intertwined into all aspects of society. The moments spent in school singing about my culture and ancestors helped build my love for poetry and storytelling. In addition to singing, I started playing the guitar at an early age.

My father's guitar was my first guitar - until one Christmas when I was gifted my own. I took guitar lessons in high school, but I mainly played by ear because the music came to me naturally. With learning the guitar, I started turning my poems and stories into songs, and this became one of my hobbies. I took my guitar everywhere. It went with me to boarding school through my high school years; around the world as I got educated in Samoa, Hawaii, and the United States.

Although I loved music, it was a hobby. So, I never considered it a career path when I was younger. I loved sports too, and it began to occupy a more dominant space in my life. After my Master's in Australia, I spent some time in New Zealand, where I worked towards representing Samoa for the 2016 Olympics as a hammer thrower. Some events prevented me from flying out to Rio, and my dreams of going to the Olympics were suddenly dashed. This left me upset and heartbroken, and I returned home to Hawaii to clear my head and work through my feelings.

While I was home, I spent time with my closest friend, who I had not seen in a long time. That Wednesday, we went to dinner, and she encouraged me to look on the bright side of things. "Everything happens for a reason," she said, trying to cheer me up. That dinner date was ironic because it was the last time I would ever see her. She was in a plane crash the following Friday, and I never saw her again.

After the crash, we searched far and wide across the Island for evidence of the crash, but no plane wreckage or bodies were found. It was heart-wrenching and has remained a painful mystery. The search went on for weeks, but we eventually reached a point where we had to close the chapter and bring the search to an end. On the last day, friends and family members who had been involved in the search hosted a music jam session, and everyone took turns playing the guitar and singing songs to express their feelings. When the guitar came around to me, I initially felt shy, but everyone was encouraging. I had written a song to cope with the pain I was going through, and I decided to share it with the people with whom I shared a sense of loss and pain. I took a deep breath, and the words of the song came out.

My friend's mum was in tears at the end of the song, and she asked me to record the song so that she could replay it and recall the memory. Before this time, I had never attempted to record any of my songs because it had only been a hobby. However, I got help from one of the families who helped us during the search. I recorded two songs in their home studio and put them on a CD that I gave to my friend's mum for Christmas that year.

Not long after, I was asked to perform the song for my friend's "Celebration of Life." After the service, many people came up to me to say they really liked the song and asked me to consider doing more music. With this encouragement, I looked up schools in California and came across Cre8 Music Academy. The Academy required music submissions as they only admitted students of a certain music calibre. At this point, I had only recorded the two songs I had done for my friend, so I emailed the music academy one of the two songs. I realised I might not get into the academy with only one demo, so I sent another email with the second song. In the email, I explained how I had not planned to share the song because it was personal, but I had realised that music was always personal to someone. Cre8 Music Academy got back to me and asked, "Have you ever thought of your music being on TV or in a film because you are a storyteller? We would love to have you at the academy and are sending you an application form right away!" Consequently, I flew to California, had a great experience, and loved every moment of it. At the end of the course, I flew back home to Hawaii, quit my job, and returned to California to continue pursuing my interests in music.

I returned to Los Angeles in 2019 with three things; my suitcase, my guitar, and a determined mindset. Needing to survive, I got a job as a Personal Training Counsellor at LA fitness and within a short time got promoted to the position of Personal Training Director. I gradually became more engrossed at work, which took away time from my music. I was trying to find the balance between maintaining my job at the gym and investing time in my music, which had been the main reason for my move to LA. That was when COVID-19 hit.

The first case of COVID-19 in the United States was confirmed on the 21st of January 2020. This was shortly after the World Health Organization announced the new virus. As the number of cases increased, a state-wide lockdown was instituted in March 2020. Things began to unravel quickly after that: the gym I worked at was forced to close, and I went from working six days a week with hardly any time for myself to being in full lockdown mode. My flatmates returned to their home state, and I was alone in my apartment for three and half months.

I found myself far away from family, living alone in a three-bedroom apartment with nowhere to go. I felt like I had lost a sense of purpose. Losing my job, my flatmates relocating, and being unable to fly home to Hawaii took a toll on me mentally. At the same time, everyone was dealing with their internal struggles as the world battled this global pandemic. I began binge-watching Netflix and HBO to occupy my mind, but this activity did not meet my need for social interaction. Without work, my bills piled up as the gyms remained closed. I saw myself descending an emotional downhill as I tried to accept how life had seemingly come to a standstill.

I began to look for creative ways to earn an income and stay active. I started a home workout routine and helped deliver groceries to those unable to go shopping during the pandemic. This may seem small, but as the risk for elderly people dying from COVID-19 grew higher, so did their fear of going out to get their food and shopping. Others had their hands full, trying to balance work with looking after their children.

My deliveries were always received with much appreciation, and my "new normal" routine began to take shape. My day included a daily workout, home-cooked meals, and delivering groceries. Though not very exciting, my activities gave me a sense of purpose and enabled me to shift from the hopelessness that enveloped me when the lockdowns started. It was at that time that I started to work on my music again. With the lockdown bringing a slower pace of life, I had the opportunity to have my thoughts together in one place without distractions. I got new housemates who were also into music, and we listened to one another's work, providing feedback.

During this season, music pulled me through the pain

and heartaches of the police injustices happening all around the United States. The case of George Floyd, a 46-year-old black American, amongst many other names, who succumbed to the same systematic violence yet to be addressed in the country, was raging. There were vigorous protests in Los Angeles and nationwide. I and many others marched peacefully with signs in our hands, masks on our faces, and intention in our hearts. Protesting in Los Angeles is an experience I will never forget. We were shot at with rubber bullets and had to avoid tear gas and other forms of brutal intervention. It was a dangerous time to speak out; indeed, it was a dangerous time to be protesting because of the pandemic.

I wrote music, I marched, and I educated others on the topic. The pandemic provided an opportunity for me to get back into music and heal alongside the rest of the world at my own pace.

About Kasandra

Kasandra is a music producer and singer-songwriter, educator, and community builder. She is currently the Head of Community for Feature in the blockchain industry. Kas is one of the Co-Founders of NFTs. Tips and the Team Lead for SearchLight - a community-led curatorial team that creates opportunities for artists around the world in the NFT space. Kas bridges the gap between art, tech, culture, and provenance. She brings an enthusiastic voice to new projects, ventures, and creators.

FACING THE FEARS

Sophie Booth Guyit

It started in November of 2019. The news of a novel Coronavirus outbreak in Wuhan began taking the spotlight on all media platforms. Social media and some forms of traditional mass media rolled out the numbers of people infected with COVID-19, and the death toll. Globally, it was initially seen as a 'concern' that was not out of control.

In the last quarter of 2019, Lassa fever was a public health concern in Nigeria. So, a novel virus in faraway China didn't seem like something that should overly concern us. Perhaps, we should have been more cautious.

I have always been more of an alarmist than most of my associates. So, I had already started feeling the weight of the rumours dampening my spirit. Questions and more questions: *What if it's already within our borders? If someone coughs, would I contract it? Could I go out in public and do what was necessary to keep body and soul together? Can I trust anyone around me?*

I mentioned my growing fears to a friend, and she passed them off, saying that Lassa fever was the real terror, not some far-off virus. But I wasn't put any more at ease.

In January 2020, the World Health Organisation moved the status of the new virus to a pandemic. And as though my fears were prophetic, COVID-19 became resident in Nigeria in February. More questions. *Why hadn't anyone listened and heeded the warning and acted appropriately? Who has the virus, who doesn't? No vaccine, no treatment. Who would survive, who wouldn't? Arrggghhhh!* I was running out of my mind with unanswered questions. Then, the containment measures to control the spread began.

Many months later, so much has happened. The first Nigerian casualty was the father of one of my friends. Two of my cousins contracted the virus, but they recovered. The questions and fears are still there, but something new has emerged. Faith.

At its very core, faith is belief. It could be the belief in a chosen ideal that guides daily living as one reaches for heaven from earth. Faith could be the belief to receive the unusual from heaven as evidence of the backing of a superior God. It carries us through the storms and along the shores of life.

The pandemic forced me to learn a new angle of faith - facing my fears. At the beginning of the pandemic, I was mostly always afraid. The fear almost paralysed me. I feared most especially for my family. However, seeing that my fear could not help me, I took the issue to my Father in Heaven. I remember one time I prayed:

Abba. I fear because of my past; I fear the present. And tomorrow? Would tomorrow even come in one piece?

And as I talked with my heavenly father, He taught me to trust Him despite the unanswered questions. And to do that, I had to face my fears and not let them control or paralyze me. I had to move and live each day, knowing that tomorrow would come and somehow everything would be just fine.

Having faith is not the easiest rule in the book. It is not the easiest because faith is dependent upon a higher power for everything. The questions are still unanswered, and that's just fine because I don't need them answered to live. I simply depend on God. This storm will grow quiet, but while it rages, I have faith to face the fears.

About Sophie

Sophie is a trained medical doctor who took to her own path after college, searching for a niche in preventive medicine. Sixteen years later, she is still trying to get people to be more aware of lifestyle choices that improve quality of life. She believes food is the ultimate medicine and enjoys creating new healthful recipes with her toddler serving as her sous chef.

Sophie loves writing, especially about her understanding of Abba (God) and hopes someday soon to own a Lifestyle Wellness Paradise in Abuja where she currently resides with her family.

A HUNDRED DAYS AND COUNTING

Teejay Fehr

Life Before Lockdown

In early March 2020, several Filipinos in my church community decided to share a piece of our culture with our friends in Vancouver, Canada. We decided to host a Boodle Fight Dinner on Sunday, March 8th. A Boodle Fight is a community meal spread out on banana leaves, eaten with nothing but your hands! It was started by the Philippine military a long time ago to build love and a feeling of community among the people. Eventually, others outside of the army began doing it independently, and a tradition was born.

I still remember the day of the Boodle Fight. It was early spring; the city had that escalating, lively vibe, which, to my mind, perfectly matches the excitement of flowers waiting for their full bloom. Friends and strangers gathered around two big, long tables, put on gloves, exchanged jokes, shared tales of heritage, and caught up on one another's lives. My husband and I had our fill of rice, seafood, pork, and assorted veggies.

After we ate, the group was about to begin a karaoke party. Even though karaoke is a form of creative expression that Filipinos would rarely turn down, my husband and I had to leave because one of our close friends was debuting his new short film a few blocks up Homer Street.

I still remember how much awe I felt for the passion of those in attendance. We all cheered for joy as the credits rolled, so happy with the hilarious movie we had just watched. Before capping off our night, my husband, Jon, and I visited another friend, reminding him to attend a small birthday party we had prepared for that Wednesday.

The Wednesday party was wonderful because we had a group of our close friends in one place. We were so happy and couldn't imagine any drastic changes in our way of life. However, the next day, I started coughing and showing signs of a cold. On Friday, we called 811, Canada's health line, to talk to a nurse that would help me assess if I needed to test for COVID-19. It was then that the reality of the pandemic sunk in for us.

No one expected the world to shut down as it did. But in a matter of days, everything changed. Canada went into her first stages of lockdown on Monday, March

16th. However, Jon and I had gone into isolation on Friday, March 13th, because I was ill.

Waiting in line to speak with a nurse on the day we called was exhausting. We got on the call at about six in the morning and stayed on hold for over two hours. Finally, our turn came, and I explained my symptoms. The nurse said we should self-isolate for fourteen days since Jon had recently been out of the country. So, that's what we did. As at the time of writing this, we had isolated for one hundred days.

At first, it wasn't so bad. I was happy to have my husband working from home and being near me every day. But as the days turned to weeks, and we started to see things like toilet paper and hand sanitiser vanish from grocery stores, we began to get discouraged. How long would this last? The worst part was worrying about my family in the Philippines. They were thousands of miles away, and many of them worked in the medical field, including my brother. I called him and found out that his hospital in Mindanao had a serious problem. They lacked Personal Protective Equipment (PPE), like masks, goggles, face shields, and gowns. My brother, a doctor, had to use the same mask day after day.

I wanted to help my brother and his hospital, but I wondered what I could do from Canada? Jon thought he might have some success reaching out to leaders in the Philippines and even found the email for Vice President Leni Robredo. He contacted her, asking if she could expedite aid to the southern part of the country. She promised she would do what she could, but the PPEs were in high demand all over the country.

Collective Effort Brings About Hope

The pandemic has made people from all corners of the world fear their chances of survival from this unknown pandemic that had caused societal and economic distress. My country, the Philippines, was not doing well. Some leaders like VP Robredo and Mayor Vico Sotto were very successful in their efforts, but there seemed to be so many barriers to getting support from other leaders. As a result, distrust of the government significantly increased, causing more division within the population. More devastating was the ostentatious display of disorganization and the lack of skills and sense of foresight among the many leaders of my country. If I had focused on the political climate of the Philippines, I would have succumbed to hopelessness.

After I realised that I could not focus on the political

authorities, I turned to God for comfort. I turned to Him and thanked Him for all the great things He had done. This was essential for me to find hope. I needed to surrender everything (including my fears and worries) to Him and stop focusing on my negative reality. This change of perspective helped me eventually develop a plan to help my brother and his team.

As I mentioned earlier, we have an incredible community of friends here in Vancouver. Thinking about them gave me the idea of seeing if any of them would be willing to help. So, Jon and I put together a fundraiser on Gofundme to try and raise money to buy protective equipment and have it shipped to the Philippines. Our friends and family shared the Gofundme and donated till we were able to raise $1200. After adding funds from our pocket, we were ready to buy some PPE and ship them to the Philippines.

Finding and purchasing quality equipment turned out to be much more difficult than we expected. Personal Protective Equipment were in high demand, and the prices were over-inflated. After spending a considerable amount of time searching various vendors on Alibaba Express, we procured some items. There were some complications, but thankfully the items arrived at the hospital, and my brother and his colleagues could get the protection they needed.

After this, I noticed a surge of people taking the initiative to help others in their own ways. I have friends residing abroad just like me, and they have done what they could to collect food and purchase supplies for their home countries. A friend in Australia rallied her co-workers to buy masks and send them to my brother's team. Through all this, I realized that no matter how small a single person's contribution, we could survive the situation if we all came together. I will never forget how incredible it was to see all the friendly messages coming in from friends and family willing to contribute to this cause. It was an encouragement to me to see that even though we were isolated and distant, our community was still there, waiting and willing to extend help to one another and the ones we love.

About Teejay

Teejay Fehr is an Early Childhood Teacher who has academic and professional experiences in the Philippines and Australia. Due to the pandemic and the unique needs that families encounter at home, with the help of friends and former colleagues, she was able to start an online consultancy called The Teaching Partners.

She recently moved to Canada, where she married young adult fantasy author, J.R. Fehr. They have a cat named Marshmallow; they home share with a man with a disability. They have enjoyed each other's company more than ever since social restrictions were implemented.

PIVOTING TO NEW OPPORTUNITIES

Tope Sogbuyi

Finding my essence

I am a Nigerian; I was born and raised in South London. Despite my upbringing, I was always aware of the subtle racial tension present when I interacted with people. The pressure was everywhere, my professional affairs not left out. I had studied and worked hard and landed myself a prize job at a renowned accounting firm. As time passed, I felt choked, encumbered, and unable to pursue my dreams. My frustrations were a combination of seemingly inconsequential things and bigger dividing issues. My jaw ached permanently because of the awkward grins I had to hold every time I explained how my braids stayed in, what I was eating for lunch - that yam was not potato, or the difference between a plantain and a banana. My face hurt from biting my tongue in order not to rock the boat when my team members did not know about black history month. Once, I left work with a headache after hearing a senior colleague say that the Grenfell survivors did not deserve to be provided new build properties in Chelsea and Kensington Borough because she was unable to afford living there, even on her full-time salary. I was fed up with having to tone down my essence. I realised I needed to be free; I needed to feel happiness every day and be appreciated. I also needed to ensure that I enabled people around me to shine and live their best lives.

I needed time off to think through what I wanted out of life and my career, so I decided to take a career break. In January 2018, I quit my corporate job in one of the big four accounting firms in the United Kingdom (UK) and began a self-exploration journey. I gave deep thought to what I enjoyed doing and what ventures I could launch to use my skills and experience. In August 2018, I started @Ginandgist, a social events platform showcasing talent and brands (especially within the black community). I was new in the events space, but this new venture thrived. I was selling out tickets and building a brand that received positive feedback and high engagement. I was earning more from a single event than I did in a month. More importantly, I was happy doing something I enjoyed. I started out doing my events quarterly, but @Ginandgist quickly grew into hosting monthly events with increasing demand.

In February 2020, I launched the first monthly urban quiz night with a new vibe, a new venue, and a new day of the week. It was relatively successful; however, March's event would dictate how much success it was. I had paid for professional flyers (up to this point, I had done everything myself). I was convinced that March 29th would be a fantastic night, and I looked forward to implementing the lessons learnt from February's launch.

While I was promoting the event, the news had been mentioning a flu-like virus that had spread from China and was causing deaths amongst the elderly and individuals who had pre-existing medical conditions. The UK had recorded a few deaths, but it was nothing compared to the numbers from China. So, when Boris Johnson, our prime minister, announced a nationwide lockdown on March 23rd 2020, it was almost unexpected and something I had never experienced before.

Following the unexpected announcement of a national lockdown, I had to cancel my event, refund all customers, and stop all social gatherings for the foreseeable future. I was suddenly unemployed without any source of income. Forced to stay at home, I was depressed from the daily announcement of death tolls, analysing the worrisome economic impacts of the pandemic, and stricter physical distancing rules. I almost regretted leaving the 'comforts' of full-time employment. How was I going to feed my son and keep a roof over my head?

I had to pivot fast if I would survive the pandemic. So, my instincts kicked in, and I remembered a project I had started while still employed. I called it @thecareersclinic (Career Clinic). It is a platform I created to help people gain employability skills. I realised that this service had gained a new layer of importance within the context of the pandemic because people were losing their jobs at a devastating rate and would need to start over. I was experienced enough to equip them with the skills required to apply for new roles. I quickly revived the concept and forged ahead. Over the following months, I rolled out my services and had consultations with clients via different online platforms. Many of my clients were women between eighteen and twenty-five years, and small businesses looking for the right talent.

Through the Career Clinic, I helped my clients improve their employment prospects by working with them to enhance their curriculum vitae, cover letters and maintain confidence during interviews with prospective employers. An essential aspect of this was helping people discover and appreciate the skills they had.

Some of my clients had not worked before or had been stay-at-home moms who were trying to get back to work.

Initially, some of my clients felt they had no skills; this is not true when you look beneath the surface. Take, for example, a stay-at-home mum who has raised a family. She may not have loads of corporate work experience but would have people and time management skills, which could be transferred to work in any industry.

As time went on, demand for my services at the Career Clinic grew. However, the reality of the pandemic also hit hard. Many in need of my services could not pay because of the pandemic's impact on their livelihood. I began doing 45 minutes free sessions for people affected by COVID-19, but I also knew that I needed to pivot again and get a job that would give me a regular income. So, I started applying for jobs until I got a contract appointment with a firm where I could work remotely. This was quite beneficial, as having a steady income gave me funds to invest in the Career Clinic, enabling me to invest in people.

It has been over a year since the pandemic hit, and our lives have changed. In the UK, especially in London, there have been long periods of lockdown. I have been on emotional highs and lows. I have spent more time with my eight-year-old son than I have done since he was six months old. However, I missed the trips and vacations abroad I had hoped to take him on.

One of my key lessons in this period is that life is too short. So every morning now, I am thankful for the opportunity to see another day. I knew that every day is a privilege, but the pandemic has put it in perspective. As morbid as it may sound, tomorrow is not promised to anybody; only the legacies we lay will last. The pandemic got me thinking about my legacy and what I would leave behind for my son.

I am learning to appreciate the people around me more. My elderly mother has the habit of randomly calling me on Saturdays to take her to Peckham (a market hub in London that has shops with Nigerian goods). In the past, I would complain about how I was tired and did not have enough notice. Now, I see these requests as an opportunity to spend quality time with her and other people I know and love. It is a privilege to get to see and spend time with people you love and a privilege to have someone reach out to you for help. In all, I have learned to be more generous with giving my time, skills, and money to the people around me. This has been very rewarding.

About Tope

Tope is a 33-year-old employment engagement advisor from London and mother to an amazing 9-year-old. Tope enjoys socialising, eating out at new restaurants, and watching Korean dramas.

Tope has developed an entrepreneurial flare and has launched her own businesses during the pandemic. However, she can't wait to travel freely without the fear of catching COVID.

RIDING THE WAVES OF ADVERSITY

Emem Opashi

I learnt early in life that the ability to adapt to change is an essential survival skill. As the daughter of a Nigerian diplomat, my family was constantly on the move. I grew up in several countries, and though I learned so much about the world, it also meant that I could never really call anywhere home. In many instances, I had only just got to settling down and making friends when we had to leave and start all over again! So, I learnt to accept change as part of life and quickly adjust.

The ability to accept change worked for me as I raised three children with different personalities and needs. It has also helped me navigate the waters of doing business in Nigeria, which is riddled with uncertainty. I describe myself as an unconventional educator who loves helping people view education through a different lens. Through my work as a coach, consultant, and course creator, I help educators establish more responsive structures to parents' needs. With lots of grit and determination, I have created a niche in early childhood education in Nigeria. I founded the Sage School and School Resource Center, both in Abuja, and pioneered an early childhood education model that has been successfully adopted by some public and private schools in northern Nigeria and some other parts of the country.

As 2020 began, I reflected on my business ventures, and I realized I needed to do things differently. I wanted to run a leaner business model and look for more ways to utilize online platforms to achieve better results. In January, I flew into Nigeria from the United Kingdom to discuss the planned change with my staff. We began mapping out a phased approach to this journey. Little did I realize at this point that the world as we knew it was about to change.

Fast forward to March 2020. COVID-19 had spread around the globe, and Nigeria was not spared. Suddenly, complete lockdowns were instituted in Lagos and Abuja, and the government ordered all schools to close. At this time, I had returned to the UK, but my husband was caught in the lockdown in Nigeria.

Before Nigeria's lockdown, I had been planning our annual conference - Annual School Needs Expo (ASNE), which usually held in Abuja. It would be the

10th anniversary of ASNE, and I had planned to celebrate with a bang. However, it became clear that the celebration wasn't going to happen. As a realist, I also took stock of the evolving financial situation of the Sage School and School Resource Center. We had been hit early and hard by the pandemic because we derived our income from fees paid for services when in session. As week after week passed and the number of COVID-19 cases continued to rise, the possibility that schools would soon be allowed to reopen became dimmer, and finances continued a downward plunge.

So again, the need to quickly accept change and make needed adjustments to survive became obvious. I needed to fast-track the implementation of a leaner business model, which meant I had to cut my staff strength by over fifty per cent. I had been working with a lovely team of talented people, and some of them had been with me for years, so this was very heart-wrenching for me. I braced myself for the difficult conversations I knew I had to have with my staff. With my advisory board, I went through every job role and asked if it was essential at this time or not to determine who would stay and who would go. I got ready for a zoom meeting with my staff to relay the news. I also rallied our reserves to pay almost full salaries that April despite not making any income that month. During the zoom meeting, I broke the news to them and held my breath, expecting hell to be let loose. To my surprise and their credit, they received the news with more resilience and grace than I expected. It was emotional watching them blowing me kisses and being grateful for the journey so far as we said our goodbyes. I still keep in touch with those I let go and try to involve them whenever I have short-term roles.

I would say that despite the adversity, this has also been a time of opportunity and significant personal growth. As a coach and consultant, I supported schools to develop their virtual early childhood learning programs, which stretched my creativity. I still convened the 2020 edition of ASNE, which was a successful virtual event. It turned out to be a rallying point for other business owners in the education sector who were also learning to deal with the sudden challenges thrown at them. We had our widest audience participation ever and had a renowned International Education Coach speak at the event for free! On the home front, I spent more time with my children than I had in recent years, and we enjoyed weekly family facetime meetings with my hubby. I also finished writing my first book!

One of my biggest lessons this period is appreciating

the things one easily takes for granted, such as family, going out with friends, and even breathing! I have also realized we don't need many things we clutter and complicate our lives with. Right now, I am in a place where I am making every day count while riding on the waves of the crisis to make myself stronger.

About Emem

Emem, also called the Unconventional Educator, is an Education Management consultant and Organization-Relations coach. In over 23 years, she has helped thousands of key players in the public and private sector education ecosystem to easily access relevant tools, resources, and solutions whilst leveraging the right network to help them achieve their corporate objectives.

She is the Convener of one of the most dynamic, global, and long-standing education platforms, The Annual School Needs Expo (ASNE), now going into its 11th year! Her first published book, *In Quest of the Perfect Education,* is a must-have for educators and parents alike. It has been purchased across four continents since its launch in July 2020.

Dividing her time between the UK and Abuja for the

past two and half years, she has successfully managed a team of over thirty people remotely. She has used this skill to create online courses and programs to equip business owners run better systems and processes. Emem is married with three grown children. She enjoys traveling, music, fitness, reading, fashion, food, and exploring educational systems globally.

Connect with her:
www.instagram.com/ememopashi
Also: @ememopashi everywhere!

THE NEW NORMAL - "LIVING ONLINE"

Eni Ayeni

Life before the pandemic

I am a busy woman. I describe myself as triangular. A significant part of my life revolves around my home, my job, church, and business. I also spend some time shopping and stocking my storehouse.

At the beginning of 2020, work included being the team lead at Community Advancement Initiative for Self-Reliance (CAI4SR), an NGO I had established with my husband in 2009. I also wanted to grow my customer base for my multi-level marketing business. As the vision executor for the NGO, I put the utmost effort into coordinating and running the organisation.

In keeping with this practice, I led the CAI4SR team through a strategic review process. We had drafted and completed our five-year strategy document. With this document as a guide, we were running with the mandate to achieve our goals for 2020. This was important: the NGO had clocked ten years, and a new dimension of the vision had been birthed. A vision centre, a place where people could get their eyes screened for free, was established. After the eye screening, some people received free medicated glasses, while others got theirs at a discounted price that helped to keep the centre running.

Disruption of Plans

The vision centre was embarking on an aggressive free eye screening project within and outside Osun state. The target was to screen at least fifty thousand people before the second quarter of the year. Then came COVID-19, disrupting everyone's plans. My team and I started working from home even before total lockdowns were imposed. I closed the office immediately because conducting refraction requires close contact with clients, and I did not want to risk my team members' lives. Regrettably, I could not help clients who needed our services due to the pandemic. My business was affected so much that prospecting and sales went low; my career pursuit came to a halt; my educational advancement was also put on hold. It was as if I had arrived at a dead end. As an active person who does so many things simultaneously, I was stuck at home for several months.

Though I worked from home, the arrangement was fraught with many challenges. My routine consisted of waking up early in the morning, taking a shower, having breakfast, and working. I would sit in front of my computer in my room, and there came the challenge – having my bed in ready reach was a big temptation. I battled with going back to bed instead of working. It was an abnormal situation. I was office sick for the first two weeks of staying at home. It took me a long time to adjust.

With everybody stuck at home, everyone who lived in my house adapted to the routine of sleeping, waking up, eating three square meals, and sleeping again. Expenditures on food and other household items rose while salaries were slashed, and some benefits excised. The period brought me to the point of deep thought about my future, family, career, and business. I did a lot of brainstorming on how CAI4SR would stay afloat amidst the pandemic and after.

Taking Life Online

I began to look up ways to keep myself engaged and increase my income even while at home. I explored different ways to remain connected to my church, do business and earn an income. Through the period, my faith continued to be an anchor and stabilising force. I stayed connected to the church through online services and spent a lot of time reading scriptures and praying. My understanding of my spiritual and kingdom assignment increased astronomically. This contributed to my stability from all the anxiety and fear. I knew that the pandemic was a phase that would pass.

The church was not the only thing that moved online for me. As an entrepreneur involved in multi-level marketing, some of my business revolved around organising on-ground training, mentoring and client prospecting events. However, with the pandemic's emergence, I was forced to explore virtual channels for conducting presentations, prospecting, closing, and following up with clients. It was fun for me, and I got a lot of sign-ups during virtual meetings. These virtual meetings, I have decided, have come to stay.

I also moved online to pursue some personal development. I attended webinars, enrolled in online courses, and joined groups on Facebook. I listened to Tony Robbins, Business Mastery, and Advance Your Reach by Pete Vargas. These inspired me to start a blog and new YouTube channels for myself and CAI4SR. I also got online mentors who taught lots of inspiring things. I started having virtual meetings with my staff.

We used the internet to plan and discuss how to launch out once the lockdown ended. A vital lesson of the period was that "businesses without online presence may not survive."

The way we process, take actions before, during, or after a negative or positive incident is determined by our mindset. It determines how we recover from a crisis. If we have a negative attitude, we end up falling victim to that crisis. On the other hand, if we have a positive mindset, we will overcome the problem.

The pandemic has caused and brought defeat to many people, especially those who lost their loved ones, jobs, businesses and have experienced low sales. The world also saw an increase in gender-based violence, sexual assault, and many other issues. However, some people benefited by going out of their comfort zone to embark on new projects and ventures in the extraordinary realm. These people have achieved tremendous feats in the most unprecedented times. They have turned their difficult circumstances into stepping-stones that have inscribed their names in the legacy of our times.

About Eni

Eni is a public health professional and founder of Community Advancement Initiative for Self-Reliance, an NGO based in Osogbo, Osun state. She is an "Eye Health" advocate and wants to help people see well and live better lives.

She is married to Dr. Benjamin Oluropo Ayeni, a wonderful and supportive man.

FINDING PURPOSE IN CHAOS

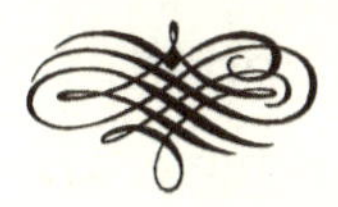

Halima Musa-Bakwunye

I have always had supportive men around me. First, my father: he firmly believed in educating and empowering girls. He made me believe that I could achieve anything and realise all my dreams in life. This belief has carried me through many of life's challenges and has seen me grow in my career as a lawyer. Next, my husband: I am lucky to have a husband who supports and encourages me in all my endeavours.

Looking around, I saw that many women did not have the confidence and courage to pursue their dreams because they lacked support. I also realised that it is vital for children to have the right mindset and foundation to succeed in life. I found only a few opportunities in my environment to nurture children and women to build the confidence and skills to succeed in life. Musing on all of these led me to start an NGO called Pavilion of Hope Foundation. My vision was to create an inclusive umbrella where cultural and religious differences did not constitute barriers to getting needed support.

Also, as a lawyer, I realised that I could channel my passion for humanitarian activities through my legal profession. So, I created a group on Facebook known as Free Legal Advice Nigeria (FLAN) but now renamed as 'Naija Laws with Halima'. I conceived the online group as a part of Pavilion of Hope Foundation. What we do in Naija Laws with Halima is to give free seminars and legal advice for a minimum of three days and a maximum of five days every month.

In a few years, the Pavilion of Hope Foundation grew from a Facebook page to hosting several live events for women and children throughout the year. Located in Satellite Town Lagos, our community-based projects are focused on education, empowerment, and enlightenment. In addition to our annual competition for kids, we successfully introduced and hosted a Mathematics competition, a poetry festival, and several skill acquisition classes for children and the youths in 2019. I loved the opportunities to interact with the children one-on-one and looked forward to rerunning the mile in 2020. I scheduled our second annual Mathematics competition for May 2, our second annual Poetry Festival for October 1, and our tenth yearly children's competition (creative writing, art, and dance) for December 2020 was booked and looking good. We started preparing for these events early.

Suddenly, the COVID-19 pandemic started unravelling in Nigeria. A total lockdown was enforced, restricting all movements in Lagos in mid-March 2020. It seemed like everything on fast gear was brought to a screeching halt. We cancelled the mathematics competition, much to my disappointment and that of the children. As the days of the lockdown turned into weeks and the number of COVID-19 cases continued to increase, I realised that I needed to figure out if Pavilion of Hope would continue rendering its services. On the other hand, Naija Laws With Halima was fine because it had always been an online project.

I had kept in touch with some families and children who participated in our previous events. These interactions brought my attention to a new growing need. A lot of families earned income from small businesses and they had been hit hard by the restrictions imposed by the lockdown. Many of them were struggling to meet their needs; they were not assured of their next meal. I realised that though our services requiring physical gatherings could not hold, we could reach out to these children and their families in another way. We could reach out to them by providing palliatives to cushion the effect of the lockdown.

Staff and members of the foundation donated what they

could. Since the lockdown had hit almost everyone's pocket to some extent, this was not an easy task. However, another NGO, Rakia Anephy Balogun Foundation reached out to us and made our burdens lighter. Our discussion resulted in teamwork that led to one of the biggest palliative distributions in our community in Satellite Town. We were able to reach over one hundred families with various food items.

The turnout for the support was much more than we expected, with people already beginning to gather hours before the scheduled time. This was a bit tasking, as we had to figure out how to ensure physical distancing through the process. In the end, the response and appreciation from the beneficiaries of the distribution of palliatives were heart-warming. Although I can't claim the palliative drive met all the needs in the community, the opportunity to do what we could and put smiles on people's faces around amounted to something.

We continued to reach out to the less privileged children, giving and distributing educational materials, from exercise books, pencils, colouring pens, and snacks at remote locations like Ade Oshodi, Ijegun, Satellite Town, and my hometown, South Ibie, Edo state. On August 10-16, 2020, we organised our first online social learning camp for the kids. We taught them creative writing, creative art and gave motivational talks. We also organised a very small class for kids who could not attend the online camp. All our other projects in 2020, were held online. We successfully hosted our second annual poetry Festival and our tenth annual children's competition via our Facebook and Instagram pages on October 1 and December 20, 2020, respectively.

The pandemic has been a period of growth for me, as I learned to do things differently to keep moving. Sometimes, we get overwhelmed by the seemingly extensive efforts required to help others out of difficult circumstances that we opt to do nothing. However, I realised from the palliative drive that we may not need much to help others. Every little help counts, and putting all our widows' mites together can and does make a difference.

For the Pavilion of Hope Foundation and Naija Laws With Halima, we will continue to grow as we explore new ways of doing things and making impacts. That is all we can do. Taking it one step and one day at a time, we look to a future where COVID-19 is history.

About Halima

Halima (LLB, BL, LLM), is a lawyer and a humanitarian. She is a co-founder and chairman of Pavilion of Hope Foundation, and the creator of a group on Facebook known as Naija Laws With Halima. She is driven by the passion to make positive impact in the lives of kids, youths, and women. All her projects for children are free, with no fees. She loves to read, write and travel. She is married and currently lives in Lagos State, Nigeria with her husband and kids.

DRAWING STRENGTH FROM HUMAN CONNECTIONS

Ololade Tunji-Abiola

I arrived in Canada sometime in September 2019 for my postgraduate studies. I gradually adjusted to my life as a postgraduate student and caregiver for my nearly three-year-old daughter and my eight-year-old son. It was challenging, but I was beginning to balance my schoolwork and caring for my children. I had learnt to live with Manitoba's harsh weather, walking my son to school during its most trying weather conditions from September through January. Often, our five minutes seemed like a long journey as we trumped through the thick snow or waded through the rains. Apart from dealing with the vagaries of nature, I often had to keep up with my daughter's unpredictable demands to be carried instead of staying in her stroller or walking.

As I adjusted to my new life as a schooling mum, I drew strength from my faith. As a Christian, I believe that God wants me to be wherever I find myself in life. I am not one to dwell on self-pity or complain about life's circumstances. So, I was more thankful for the opportunity to be schooling than focused on the challenges of caring for my children. My faith bolstered me when I experienced a delay securing space in a daycare for my daughter. Canada has a highly competitive pre-school system that puts children on a waiting list till vacancies are available. I was blessed with great support from the academic environment where I was pursuing my studies. On days when I could not secure a babysitter to watch my daughter while I attended my lectures, one of my professors would gladly take up the task of babysitting. This arrangement was helpful, but I still felt the burden of childcare as I often had to dash away from school to get my son once school closed. It was challenging to meet up with my schoolmates or hang out after classes because I had to rush home to care for my children. However, despite the challenges, I was thankful for the opportunity to acquire new skills. I was also very grateful to have a husband who supported my dreams back home in Nigeria.

I was looking forward to seeing my husband and older daughter when COVID-19 struck. We had planned for my husband and older daughter to meet the other children and me for a family holiday in the first quarter of 2020. I had not seen my older daughter since I started my studies seven months earlier, and I longed to finally have the family together in one place after such a long separation. However, as COVID-19 registered its presence worldwide, our carefully laid holiday plans began to fall apart. The first indication of this was when Canada closed its borders to curb the spread of the virus. Due to the new border restrictions, I would not be allowed to return to Canada if I ventured to travel out of the country at that time because of the nature of the visa I had.

As it turned out, my husband and daughter could not travel out of Nigeria because our beloved country also suddenly went into lockdown mode in March 2020. The virus had dealt me a nasty blow, and I felt terrible that my first daughter's hope of seeing me was dashed. She did not have to go through this experience. Although I talked and face-timed with her a lot, I could feel that it was never quite enough.

My school schedule changed due to the physical distancing guidelines put in place, and our classes were moved online. Although this made childcare more manageable since I was home with my younger daughter and son, my children had to be quiet anytime I attended classes online. It initially felt strange that my children had to speak in whispers in their own home, but they soon got used to it. I was thankful for that period because I did not need to figure out where to keep my younger daughter.

My greatest challenge during the pandemic was navigating through the initial chaos and the panic of people around me. The fears were palpable, and an experience at the mall captured the depth of people's fear. One morning, I caught the 9 a.m. bus as I usually did once a week to get my groceries before the daily rush of other shoppers. On the bus, I mentally scanned through my list and braced myself to shop as quickly as possible, hoping to return home within the hour. As I neared my stop, I was surprised to see a very long queue through the bus window. I had never seen such a crowd shopping at this time. It occurred to me that people were stockpiling and panic buying. I was frustrated; I could barely get all the items I wanted from my shopping list. The worst part was that there was hardly any tissue paper on the shelf. This singular event clarified how the pandemic would significantly impact our lives and the possibility that things would not be normal for a while. Or how could one explain the scarcity of the commonest of all items - tissue paper? It was so bad that tissues had to be rationed by the malls to remain available for those who needed them most.

In the face of these life-changing events, my faith became the pillar upon which I leaned. More so, the pandemic made me look inward and reassess my relationships with those around me. I realised that I needed to do better in reaching out to family, friends, colleagues, acquaintances, and people around me. Before the pandemic, I had been so engrossed with schoolwork and caring for my children - I hardly knew any of my neighbours. With the pandemic's restrictions, the estate managers for my apartment building placed strict restrictions on movement, such that no visitors were allowed in. This made me feel isolated, as the few visitors I ever got did not live in the building.

With this realization, I became intentional in interacting with my neighbours. As I interacted more with my neighbours, I discovered an invaluable support system. With the kids at home and no available babysitting, I found that I could not handle things independently as I had done before the pandemic. This challenge came up in discussions with my neighbours, and I was lucky to find a neighbour who could check in on the children whenever I had to leave the house.

The pandemic has been life-changing. It forced me to question and rethink the way I do things. I have taken a break from my busyness and become more conscious of the things and people around me. In doing this, I have learnt better to appreciate the value of human connections and interactions. I have experienced the humane side of the people around me.

About Ololade

Ololade is married with three adorable children. She works as an advertising agency administrator. When not being a wife, mother, or administrator, she enjoys curling up with a good suspense novel or trying out a new food recipe.

SILVER LINING TO DARK CLOUDS

Abiola Adimula

Achieving Dreams

Over the years, I have pursued and accomplished many of my dreams and aspirations. I firmly believe that, with diligence and hard work, one can achieve whatever one wants to do. I have applied this belief as I built my family and established my law firm, which marked its 25th anniversary in 2020. This was also my guiding principle as I charted the course for a career change well into my fourth decade of life. After working for over 20 years as a professional lawyer and building my law practice, I got a chance to take a career detour into academia and research, and I decided to take up the challenge. I completed my PhD in 2014, 22 years after obtaining my first degree, and I am now a senior lecturer at the Centre for Peace and Strategic Studies at the University of Ilorin, Ilorin, Nigeria.

Though I had achieved many of my aspirations and ticked off many things from my bucket list, one thing I had been unable to do was obtain a certificate from

Harvard University. I admire Harvard and have always wanted to get a degree or certificate from there. However, my busy schedule made it quite impossible to pursue this dream. I simply could not take time off work and from all my responsibilities to get this done.

When the first cases of COVID-19 hit Nigeria, I was in the middle of preparations for two events. The first event was my brother's wedding. I am Yoruba, and our wedding ceremonies are colourful and boisterous events that require lots of planning and preparations. A key part of Yoruba wedding preparations is choosing and distributing the Aso Ebi, which family and friends wear, and I was taking charge of this. The second event I was preparing for was teaching a short course for executive participants from various government agencies in Nigeria.

When lockdowns were instituted across the country as part of measures to combat the spread of COVID-19, these two events were suspended abruptly. I saw plans for my brother's big boisterous Yoruba wedding quell down into a small guest list, and I realized things were not going to be the same for a long while. As almost everything came to a halt, I realized that the times called for a different approach towards tasks at hand

and a deliberate refocus on opportunities instead of challenges. This enabled me to move forward despite the odds and continue my research work and attain my long-held dream of obtaining a certificate from Harvard.

As I tried to look for opportunities to continue my research despite the lockdown, I discovered the beauty of collaboration. Before COVID-19, I had personally handled collecting all the data for my research. This had required multiple trips to Internally Displaced Persons (IDP) camps in North-East Nigeria because that was my research focus. With the lockdown, I found myself stuck in Ilorin, more than 1,000 kilometres away from north-eastern Nigeria, at a point when I needed to get more data from the field. It looked like my research work would stop as I couldn't travel to the area like I usually would. Determined to continue my work anyway, I reached out to a colleague who lives in the north-east to discuss the possibility of us working together; he agreed. We struck up a collaboration that involved him collecting the data needed for that time. The outcome of that collaboration was two research papers submitted for publication in international journals.

A combination of two fallouts from the COVID-19

lockdown enabled me to achieve my dream of obtaining a certificate from Harvard. One was I suddenly had lots of time on my hands. All my proposed conference trips were cancelled, and all school activities at the university temporarily stopped. Having this much free time felt very strange because my busy routine left me with little or no time for myself for many years. The second was that I had to learn to use online platforms more efficiently to get things done. This opened my eyes to the world of online schooling. Emboldened by my increased confidence navigating the internet, I enrolled for an online course in Child Protection offered by Harvard University. This placed me on an intense 15-week journey which involved loads of reading, assignments, and midnight candle burning. In the end, it was all worth it as I finally achieved my dream and held my Harvard certificate in my hands!

As my husband would jokingly remark, "Abiola, you have used this lockdown profitably." My big takeaway from this period is that setbacks in life can often be used to our advantage. So many things are possible if we learn to focus on opportunities in the storm.

About Abiola

Ruth Abiola Adimula (PhD) is the principal partner of Biola Adimula & Co., a firm of Legal Practitioners established in 1995 with head office in Ilorin, Kwara State, Nigeria, and a senior lecturer at Centre for Peace and Strategic Studies, University of Ilorin, Ilorin, Nigeria. She obtained her PhD in Peace and Development Studies in 2014, LL.M 2004 (Obafemi Awolowo University, Nigeria), and LL.B. in 1992 (Ahmadu Bello University, Zaria, Nigeria).

She is the President of Commonwealth Scholars and Fellows Alumni Association, Nigeria and the Secretary, Board of Trustees; the National Publicity Secretary, Society for Peace Studies and Practice, Nigeria; Peace Ambassador, Institute for Economics and Peace, Sydney (2018) and a Member Assessor Association of Commonwealth Universities Grant Selection Panel, London, United Kingdom.

She is married to a University Don - Prof. Abiodun Adimula and they are blessed with children. She lives in Ilorin, Nigeria with her family.

HOLDING ON
TO FAITH

My Hang Tran

I have wanted to be a journalist since I was a child. This desire was strong in me, and I found myself taking the right turns, going to school, registering for the right courses, and getting the right credits. Eventually, I achieved my dream and became a journalist.

My work as a journalist took me to Vietnam for about seven years. While there, I grew to dislike the way I worked, because the government censored the news. Owing to this dissatisfaction, I left journalism to work with a Non-Governmental Organisation (NGO) providing help to women and children in Vietnam. After doing this for three years, I lost my passion for the job and left the NGO to study for a master's degree in the UK.

As I neared the end of my studies in the UK, I got a job offer from the BBC. After I graduated, I moved to Bangkok, Thailand, to take up the position.

The more I have travelled and interviewed people as a

journalist, the more I have come to realize my passion for journalism is fed by the desire to help vulnerable people raise their voices and be visible, which I can do through the articles I write.

This is one of the reasons I enjoy my work in Bangkok: I have greater freedom to write and speak up for people than I did in Vietnam.

At the onset of the pandemic, I started working from home because Thailand had a lockdown that lasted about two months. Even though working from home did not pose so much difficulty in carrying out my job as it mostly involved phone interviews, I felt the effects psychologically. Sometimes I would feel a bit isolated. As a journalist, I also had to keep tabs and report on the number of COVID-19 cases and deaths. Their sufferings have also impacted me emotionally.

Despite my challenges during the first lockdown, I was determined to keep hope alive. I am a Christian, and my faith was a strong anchor in those times. I drew strength from praying and listening to sermons in my apartment.

The pandemic made me realize the importance of relationships. During the lockdown, I realized that even the little conversations an introvert has with family, friends, or colleagues, small as they are, are meaningful and foster a sense of connection. Since discovering this, I have developed closer ties with my mother and sister back home in Vietnam. Since then, we have begun exchanging calls often.

As the years pass since the start of the pandemic, the situation is still evolving. Vaccination has been rolled out across the globe, but Thailand, like many countries, struggles with access to vaccines. One can only hold on to faith and believe the pandemic will become another piece of history eventually.

About My Hang Tran

My Hang Tran is a journalist and she writes from Bangkok, Thailand. She currently works with the BBC. Previously, she worked at a newspaper in Vietnam and the World Vision (an NGO).

FINDING ME

Ademilola Bilewomo

Mind Battles

Although this book is about the pandemic and how women's lives have changed, it is more than that for me. It is my journey through rebirth and finding myself. The pandemic forced me to see and listen to myself again. That was the beginning of my trip to rediscovery.

Before the pandemic, I moved to Abuja, Nigeria's capital city, to start my life over. At that time, I had felt like a total failure because I had recently walked away from an abusive relationship. I almost lost my life; I had lost my entire savings and the investments that had taken me years to build. I had no source of income and two young children to raise. I could barely see the daily opportunities to start afresh. I was locked in the past, reflecting on what could have been if I had made different choices. I replayed every past action picking at what I could have done differently. I flogged myself a thousand times over at what a mess I had made of my entire life. I had lost my confidence and did not believe in my abilities anymore. I was a depressed woman with very low self-esteem.

The pandemic came as a rude shock. I had been trying to secure a job and restart my career in the new city; with two children to cater for, it was tough. Besides the very little information about the novel virus, I was filled with great concern as my first son has a medical condition that made him more susceptible to the virus. As such, I started practising physical distancing long before others. I had already started shielding my son even before the government announced a nationwide lockdown. However, while I was relieved that I could shield my son from danger, I was also very disturbed about my prospects of securing a job. The lockdown meant that I had to remain at home with my children because schools were closed. I was a single mom, doctor, cook, nanny, teacher, breadwinner, and job seeker.

At some point, everything was physically and emotionally draining. I was locked in my apartment for days, not venturing out of my home even for a walk. I had disengaged my housekeeper, fearing that my vulnerable son could be exposed to the virus. Visitors were not welcome, and I stopped venturing out for the business opportunities that kept me going while I navigated my career change. Without any distractions, I came to terms with the reality of the moment and the depression that had engulfed me since I moved to Abuja. I was forced into moments of silence that made me examine if I was satisfied with the way I had begun to perceive myself. My mind was a battlefield of countless interoceptive questions:

Do you want to continue living in the past, judging yourself as a failure, or would you want to look at your current situation as a window of opportunity to start life afresh?

I felt like one trapped in a deep hollow - consumed by the desire to turn back the hands of time. I wanted to escape, but I could not do so on my own. Added to this, I had encountered several rejections in the last stages of high-profile job interviews and had subconsciously internalised these rejections as a confirmation of my failures. My mind was in a state of hopelessness with no glimmer of hope in sight, so I prayed: *I cannot live like this anymore; help me!*

One morning, as I struggled through my mind battles, I received a series of WhatsApp messages from a friend and prayer buddy. She wanted me to co-author a book that focused on women's experiences during the pandemic - a beacon of hope during a gloomy period. I was surprised; I had been so demotivated by life's happenings and had come to believe that I was not good enough for certain things. It was hard for me to think that anyone could invite me to co-author a book! I was excited about the idea, and I responded in the affirmative. I later received a call from her. It was the right call, amid the state of total depression I had wallowed in. For the first time in a long time, I was hopeful.

Having someone to walk with and listening to the stories of other women did me some good. I suddenly began to experience an overwhelming joy in the whole process. The initial plan had been to finish in six months, but the book assumed its own form. Instead of having women write, we listened to their stories from across the world via the internet. It was an awesome experience, a healing and soothing balm to all the hurts I had bottled up. Each story gave me a new lease of life as I realised that we all had challenges, and the way we navigated them yielded the type of results that we got. Indeed, when life is unfair, it is left to us to determine how we view life.

My confidence was the greatest gift I got from the shared experiences with all the women we interviewed. With each interview and story shared, I realised that I could do whatever I set my heart to do, no matter the obstacles in my way.

The changes in our plans for collecting stories and reaching out to people turned on a lightbulb of ideas for my job search and how I handled my job interviews. Just like we had mapped out an alternative plan for the book, I realised that perhaps I needed to change how I approached my job search and interviews. I became more open and embraced my vulnerability. This way, I could embrace every disappointment from previous interview processes without wallowing in depression. Like the women we interviewed, I opened up to others freely. This way, I was able to share my fears with a group of four women, who had become my support group and prayer buddies during the pandemic.

My prayer buddies and I met virtually for an hour every week, and we talked and prayed about everything that troubled us. With the lockdown, our moments together became a period of sharing, confiding, and encouragement. We were five women in different seasons of our lives working through the change that the pandemic had brought on as we played our roles as mothers, wives, single parents and caregivers. These women became the voice in my head anytime I felt low, and their prayers paved the way for me to focus on the opportunities that each day held.

As I blossomed in self-confidence and focused on the possibilities of life, I was able to apply for my dream job. I worked on my mindset and focused on my goals rather than my shortcomings. Working on the book taught me that there are times when it is more important to take baby steps instead of not taking any at all. So, I re-examined my skills and kept applying to jobs and getting feedback from my interviews. I approached every job application with great determination to succeed; I reviewed my curriculum vitae and ensured that my skills matched every job I applied for. I also ensured that my cover letter showcased my wealth of experience. With every interview we conducted with our contributors to the book, I gained more perspective on conveying my thoughts accurately to others. This became very useful as I approached each job interview. I also shared my hopes and fears with my prayer buddies as I progressed in my job search. They became my solace and confidants. Together, we weathered the storm; they also looked out for job opportunities for me. Indeed, there were brief moments of sadness, but the prayers of these women kept me and still are soothing in my raging moments of confusion. Interestingly, I got two jobs around the same period. Everything happened during the pandemic.

A New Perspective

In all my challenges, I have witnessed the power of sisterhood. Through my journey, I realised that women need to tell their stories more so that others can learn from their shared experiences. And even though I am still pondering whether I should share my own story, I know that my story could be what another needs to move on with life. You see, there is just this one life, and we must all muster the courage to make the best of what we have got. Life could be unfair, but we should never remain crushed. We need to pick ourselves up and keep working.

More than a year after the pandemic began, I have now come to terms with my new reality. I have come to appreciate the road I have travelled, and I have started to use the journey as a stepping stone for better decisions. My mind is no longer a battlefield. Instead, it is filled with empowering and uplifting stories of women who have surmounted challenges and thrived in one of the most challenging moments in history.

Even though I still have down moments, I remind myself about the stories of women who have thrived even in more difficult circumstances.

About Ademilola

A mother to two energetic boys, Ademilola is daily mesmerised by the deep wisdom and sheer innocence in children's conversations. She is passionate about making positive impact, particularly for women and children, using her experience in communication as a tool for effecting positive changes.

Ademilola began her career as a journalist, and currently works in the field of communications. She lives with her two boys in Abuja, Nigeria's capital city.

Acknowledgements

We want to give a shout out to all those who helped through the making of this book.

All the wonderful women who agreed to share their stories in this book. Thank you for the time spent on video calls, drafting your stories, responding to emails, and working on the edits while getting your stories together.

Our families helped in various ways to get this done; from serving as inspiration while writing, helping with the kids when we needed space to get work done, and encouraging us to continue even when we felt like giving up.

Femi Ayodele, thank you for guiding us through the process of editing and publishing a book.

About Ademilola Bilewomo

A mother to two energetic boys, Ademilola is daily mesmerised by the deep wisdom and sheer innocence in children's conversations. She is passionate about making positive impact, particularly for women and children, using her experience in communications as a tool for effecting positive changes.

Ademilola began her career as a journalist, and currently works in the field of communications. She lives with her two boys in Abuja, Nigeria's capital city.

About Oluwakemi Akagwu

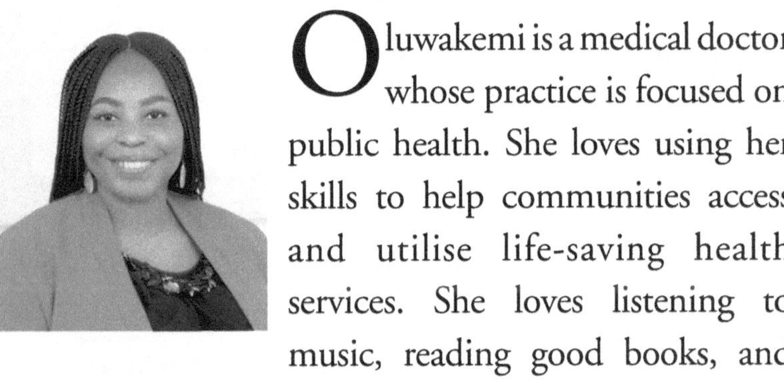

Oluwakemi is a medical doctor whose practice is focused on public health. She loves using her skills to help communities access and utilise life-saving health services. She loves listening to music, reading good books, and taking in nature's beauty while on walks or visiting new places. She lives in Abuja, Nigeria with her amazing husband, Cyril, and two kids.